FINDING OUR WAY

A GUIDE ON CARE, FINANCES AND HELPING
THROUGH THE END OF LIFE JOURNEY

LESLIE VICK

ISBN: 979-8-9905968-8-7

Published by:

Pine Book Writing

www.PineBookWriting.com

R-10225 Yonge St Suite #250, Richmond Hill, ON L4C 3B2,

Canada.

Printed in the United States of America

ABOUT THE AUTHOR

Leslie grew up knowing she had a Grandfather, Phil, who had a lifelong illness. She would watch her Grandmother Gretchen care, love, and dote on him endlessly. That was her first real example of watching a caregiver in action. The endless issues he faced with pain and walking, and then watching it take over their lives. Phil passed away at home, as Gretchen comforted him, and we all said goodbye. That is what taught her what a caregiver does. How resolute, hard, loving, and lonely it can be. Throughout her life, she had seen more of this generous side of others, giving time, love, patience, and themselves to others.

Many years later, she would assist with her own father, Tom. Tom's journey with dementia, stroke, and various surgeries led him to his passing in a nursing home. Two years later, she was the sole caregiver for her aunt Helen, who was living in another state. Ten days later, Helen passed in a hospice facility. Many various experiences have led her to help others and eventually write this guide. Caregiving to her is so much more than bedpans, prescriptions, and appointments. It is also the bills, home maintenance, and funeral planning. As you read her guide, you will find many examples and personal suggestions that made her pull her hair out, cry, and laugh!

The best part of Leslie is that she raised three successful children who cheered for her in life. And you will find her wintering in St Louis Park, MN, and summering at the lake in Cushing, MN, with her husband, Matt Farley, and her new puppers, Wallace.

SALUTATION TO THE DAWN

By: Sanskri dramatist and lyric poet **Kalidasa**

Look to this day,

for it is life,

the very life of life.

In it's brief course lies all

The realities and verities of existence,

The bliss of growth, the splendor of action

The glory of power-

For yesterday is but a dream and tomorrow is only a vision.

But today, well lived, makes every yesterday a dream of happiness.

and every tomorrow a vision of hope. Look well, therefore, to this day.

TABLE OF CONTENTS

WHY WE ARE HERE

I read somewhere that most books start by talking about the weather...it was hot, a windy day...

Well, this will not be because when we reach for this kind of guidance, and you are researching this information, the weather is not important.

The person we are helping and caregiving for starts to show signs of needing more than their basic needs are met. It really does not matter what is happening outside or what day it is. But starting a plan with them makes for an easier phase when you are having to prepare for the tough stuff ahead. I am writing this as I am going through this season with my own mother. I have helped friends and family make plans, and each person who has needed my assistance has taught me so many things about how I can help them live out their lives with less anxiety and frustration and make it less scary. Face it, none of this is fun or exciting. It is just very necessary.

1

Each journey has been so entirely different. It took my father several years to pass; too many surgeries, care facilities, and a lot of physical therapy that he hated. I have learned that you do not have to do everything that is suggested. It is okay to say enough. I am tired of treatments. It is so honorable to get to that place and be able to express it aloud. It is comforting to be the person they share it with. It is not like the movies, where there is a beautiful white nightgown and rosy cheeks, and you go to sleep and never wake up. Death can be quick and sudden. It also can be exceedingly long as they work through letting go. I witnessed my aunt, who was able to call her siblings hours after she found out it was her time, that we had exhausted all treatment. She had eight calls to make all over the US. Wow, what a gift! It was excruciating to hear her say goodbye to everyone. There is no perfect way. There is no wrong way. But you can prepare things ahead of time, have some raw conversations, and you will spare yourself so much wasted energy and get to grieving.

There is a point where the planning coincides with sadness and a word I learned to describe watching my dad slowly die. It is called "anticipatory grief" or "preparatory grief"—you are grieving while they are alive, while they are comprehending what is happening to them. I looked up the word—and it describes what you are feeling and going through so well.

The actual definition is:

Feelings of grief or loss are felt before the person passes. The person actively dying can share this same grief as you. You can be going through this for years or weeks beforehand.

Microsoft Bing-12/11/2023 Definition

This may seem overwhelming, too much, but if you do things in doses, like Mary Poppins, it does not have to be exhausting and frustrating, and you will not be pulling your hair out! If people offer to help, take them up on it. If someone wants to stop by, let them or not, but be honest. If you need to have things delivered, instead of making a fresh meal, order away. The delivery systems we have now can save so much time and money. We all want to be respectful of this chosen duty that was asked of us. We want to honor the person we care about, but we do not have to feel guilty because we had fast food or forgot to pick up their milk. It is all going to be okay because, in the end, they will pass, and they will be loved. And you got to be a part of making what time they had left easier, less complicated, and hopefully peaceful.

With all this information, you can start from any chapter, but if you can get to planning with your elderly when they are co-horrent and living independently, they will be able to make most of the decisions for themselves, and then you can just execute. Some of this information is from personal situations I have been through. Some of this is research and interviews, which are not set in stone, as states have different laws, tax laws change, and new community programs. So again, I cannot say it enough: it is a guide, a starting point, a place to say to your loved one, what is your plan? Let us decide together; you do not have to do this alone! Do you have this policy? Do you have a pension? Where do you bank? You can read this together, and that will start a hard conversation. But I guarantee it will get easier because no one is hiding or running from what can and will happen. I have used the word elderly. This can apply to anyone, like my beautiful friend who died at 50—it is really for anyone you are caregiving for or for our own personal use.

Lastly, we are in an electronic age. You can send documents through email or have Zoom calls, which helps with the process. But these are legal documents, and in a lot of cases, you will have to send an original and not a copy. Banks, investment firms, and lawyers will ask for those original signed copies, so organizing and having a paper filing system for documents is necessary. I was a trustee of an estate. That estate was across the country. I had to abide by that state's laws and regulations. I had to fly back and forth and live away from my home and, often, my everyday life. But it was a huge learning experience and a gift as I cherished my time with my aunt and helped her pass comfortably. Having the paperwork accessible and organized will definitely make things go smoother. Just because you sent it before does not mean it was received or taken care of. Keeping contact information for the people you speak to, bankers, and assistants so you have direct contact is a good plan. To this day, medical facilities still use fax machines, which is the only way to get paperwork completed in a rush. I often wrote down the day I spoke with my contact on the document I sent them. I am old-fashioned—I write things down, and I use spiral notebooks so I can go back and revisit what they said or the timing of things. All my years taking Franklin Covey classes have paid off!

I am aware that situations can be corrected, change fast, or you may be provided with inaccurate information. Be patient. Trust me, it is all a learning process—so many people and companies you will work with are understanding and knowledgeable. I often asked them if I was missing anything, if there was a question I did not ask, or just general advice.

You got this!

JUMPING IN

The caregiving part of life often starts because something significant happened, a fall, a significant diagnosis, or memory issues. And so, we are scrambling to figure out how we can help, replace, and sometimes take over someone's life and help them through this trying period. You will **never have perfection**, all paperwork completed and tidy, "T's" crossed, and "I's" dotted. But if you have some of their basic information available, it is a starting point, and you do not feel so desperate. So, by having conversations and preparing before you get to that stage, you will be able to oversee things with a clearer, more confident mind. It is always going to be stressful taking care of an adult who is dependent and refers to you for decisions. But any preparation relieves some frustration about what is coming ahead. Often, people ignore the circumstances that are in front of them. It is a lot easier to die when you have resources and a plan!

I have used the word elderly throughout the guide. This can apply to anyone, any age you are caregiving for, or for you personally.

Access-

I am starting super basic, and duh! Have a set of keys to the house, a safe box, cars, a security gate, alarms, and anything that requires a key or has a code. Nothing worse than not being able to get into their home or access their belongings. You need to have this information, as emergencies will happen. These things get misplaced or lost, and having your own set put away is "dependable." Waiting for the fire department to break down the door to get help is not how you want to find someone distressed. If they live in an apartment, do you have the building manager's contact information? You will need to have your elder's basic information, like date of birth and social security number. It helps to have insurance and Medicare/Medicaid information. We are walking into this process, so you are ready to have the deeper, harder communications you may need down the road.

Have passwords! I know we have a lot of logins and passwords, and they may get changed without you knowing, so even if they update their own and just let you know where they keep their secure electronic information, it is a lifesaver! Having access to their computer, signing on if they use one, and making a list from there, so you have a place to look. Set up a shared document so that when changes are made, it is made live and shared right away. My aunt had a little "black book" in which she had written her protected information in pencil! But I did not find this until weeks after her passing. The frustration and time wasted could have been prevented.

Suggestions on passwords:

- Banking
- Home security systems
- Social media

The Basics-

Where do they bank? A lot of our elderly bank at various places, like a credit union, because they received benefits through their job and just never consolidated to one place. Do they have a banker that they work with or a specific location? That will help if you need to go to the bank for them and help with transactions. Many benefits like Medicare and pensions are directly deposited into their household account, so knowing those deposit dates when managing bills ensures a lot of banking errors. Having a file with even a statement or access online to these accounts will save time and help with getting to cash when needing to pay expenses for them. Basic life expenses—when are bills due? Do they have a mortgage? Reverse mortgage? Do they have private health insurance? Hopefully, we will have fewer expenses later in life than in our younger years, so chances are they will mirror what you have in monthly expenses.

Do they have pensions, trusts, money markets, 401k, annuities, or other investments? Do they have beneficiaries set up, and is a copy of this information available? Certain investments have a clause that the owner can take a distribution early due to health issues without a penalty.

Have the company name, account information, and contact information if that time comes so you will be ready. Most investments need 3 or more days to sell the assets and have the money deposited or a check sent. Make a note of this so you can plan and not stress. Set up automatic transfers, allowing less chasing in the future for money when it's needed.

Titles-

Do they own vehicles, boats, campers? Some states require titles for different things, and knowing where the title is when it is time to ensure a quick sale. Otherwise, you can apply for a" transfer of title," but each state is different. I live in Minnesota, and we have a title or license for everything! i.e., golf cart, boat, trailer. When you choose to sell those items, you will have to meet the buyer at your local DMV to complete a good bill of sale. If the elder cannot physically come with you or has passed, you will need to have their death certificate, transfer on death paperwork or estate papers, and your picture ID. There are times they may still have had a lien holder on the title. You can have the lien holder (bank, credit union) sign a "lien release" and just have that with you when you go to the DMV. This shows the lien has been satisfied, and it's a good bill of sale.

If the seller has a trust, the buyer's payment must be made to the trust or the beneficiary so you can keep track of their records later. The trust will need to know where these assets are and the property's value at the time of death. Get receipts and keep that with the trust/will files, as now you have the actual value.

Note: I will go over trust and accounting later.

Animals-

Who takes care of them? What are your loved ones wishes? Does the animal have special needs?

Ask about taking their pet to the nursing home or a care facility for visits. Most facilities welcome these visitors as it helps our loved ones mentally. I can still see little Sammy running with her ears flying behind her head when she saw my dad for the first time after many weeks of not being with him.

Essential Life Box

A friend of mine has a special box that she has labeled **"essential life box."** She has several types of legal papers, statements, notes, etc. Anything she wanted her family to know when she passed. She has all the details and the system set up so they can go to one place and start. We need a starting point, without all the drama of trashing a house looking for these very necessary papers.

This box also has information on her funeral- music, readings, colors, and flowers. She has given them instruction and guidance as to what her celebration of life will look like. Her POA knows where this box is and its significance. It is a gift (real relief) she is giving her loved ones, as it is so personal and helps with decision-making. Again, when an outline or an instruction plan is completed, it helps solve so many questions.

Checklist

There are tasks, problems, and simple things that need to be taken care of, but who does what, and when? Put together a list, a chart, and designated times for how you can put together what needs to be done and who can do it. I understand that families may live out of town away from the elderly person, but they can still call to cancel or set up subscriptions, appointments, and banking. They can find transportation, professionals, and housekeeping. Be creative!

- **Medical** (health insurance, clinics, equipment)
- **Legal** (Wills, beneficiaries, titles)
- **Personal** (Banking, cleaning, subscriptions)
- **Funeral** (Policies, arrangements, family)

HAVING A DESIGNATION

Power of Attorney - POA

In the first chapter, I mentioned different legal terms or **designations**. This chapter is where we start probing and digging into harder questions. It is great to know how to get to the bank or have the password, but without them with you physically, you cannot access the accounts or get any information. Here is where we will start to get personal on ownership and how they have accounts set up and prepared. It is not enough to just be a beneficiary as that designation does not help while they are sick and alive in the hospital, needing to get their cash.

Having Power of Attorney (POA) completed paperwork and copies made will ensure business as usual while they are recovering or transitioning to different care. They can be unconscious, alive, and you are working in their best interest. There are several types that can be written up, stating medical and or personal POA. You can discuss this with an attorney as each state is different, and if they do not have this set up, it can be done quickly with no waiting period needed. Please keep copies with you, as you will need to show them when making any decisions for them.

Definition-

A power of attorney (POA) is a legal document that lets you choose someone to act for you in certain situations, such as when you are ill or away. You must be 18 years of age to be a POA on an account or health care directive.

POA - Search (bing.com) 12/11/2023

Transfer on death-TOD.

You can set this up on different accounts and assets at the time of setting up the account or purchase. This transfers the ownership of the account or asset when the person passes. The TOD is not able to write checks or check account information while the account owner is still alive or has ownership of an asset. It strictly applies after the person passes. To take over the account or asset, you would need the TOD paperwork if it is not completed right away. Have your own picture ID, SS#, and death certificate to access the account, title, or asset.

This is a quick document that can be put together and used right away with no waiting time. There are a lot of ins and outs with a TOD due to state laws, marriage, and survivorship. So do your research, and in an emergency, is your best option.

Here are some benefits of using a TOD:

- Avoids probate
- Offers tax savings
- Provides tax protection
- Offers Medicaid eligibility

Bing-12/15/2023

Definition-

A **Transfer on Death (TOD) deed** *is a legal document that allows you to designate a beneficiary who will automatically become the owner of your real property upon your death.*

TOD- Search (bing.com) 12/11/2023

Beneficiary-

Whenever I opened a bank, investment, or medical account, I was asked about adding a beneficiary. At the time I answer, sometimes I give a percentage, and I never think about it again. But life happens, a divorce, even death, and then those beneficiaries do not get changed. If the elderly did not make the changes and did not have any paperwork like a will or trust, then the most current information is what is legal.

As hard as it can be, this is a crucial time to have this conversation. A sole beneficiary could have died, and now the asset can go to probate. No one wants to see their bank account go to an old lover!

Definition-

A beneficiary allows you to direct how your belongings—such as bank balances, property, or prized possessions—should be distributed. The beneficiary has no responsibility or can make any decisions while the person is still alive. The beneficiary rights do not come into place until after the person passes.

Contingent Beneficiary-

This can be added when opening the account and in any legal form. An example would be if I were a beneficiary on my husband's account. He also has a contingent beneficiary listed, my daughter. If he passes away, she will be the sole beneficiary and have no problem accessing the funds or assets.

A backup recipient of an asset if the beneficiary is not alive.

Merriam Webster Dictionary-12/11/2023

Personal Representative (PR)-

I recently spoke with a friend, whose father had no designations listed on his real estate and personal property, when he passed away. Two of his children are living and so you would think they would automatically qualify for any assets. No- not the case, and not that easy. She had to petition the Probate Court to become her dads personal representative. That includes having the death certificate, filling out the on-line forms, making a declaration in the paper of his passing. You must have a list of all assets and have a value. She then needed a letter from her sibling, stating that she approved of her sister becoming the **PR** and that she is declining that responsibility. This process and attending the courts in person took her a good 90 days. It takes time to gather all of the paperwork needed and set up the appointment/s. There is a time constraint that you have to work with, make sure you understand what is needed beforehand.

There is an option when you have no Wills, POA, TOD, Beneficiaries and or Trusts set up. But the time, money and process are stressful and frustrating. You can go online to your County Probate Government Agency and begin the process there. Once your paperwork is approved, you will receive PR papers that need to be with you when opening up new accounts, closing accounts, and requesting documents. This is important to know that you do have a way to finalize an estate no matter how big or small. But this is not quick and again you will need to be organized and vigilant.

A beneficiary is someone to whom you want to leave assets, while a personal representative is someone named by you to oversee the distribution of your assets. The personal representative is also called the executor for a will and the successor trustee for a trust. Beneficiaries are frequently named as personal representative because they are more likely to look out for the interests of the beneficiaries than someone who is not receiving any assets from the estate.

Personal Representative- Search (bing.com) 4/23/2024

VETERAN BENEFITS

Did your loved one enroll in benefits? Were they enlisted during "active war"?

In this chapter, I will just go into general applications and what different programs they have to offer. It is always changing; it is a process to apply and has restrictions. I have contact information for several sites below to get you started.

I have several military members in my family at different branches and during different periods. My father, for all his years, after he was honorably discharged, never chose to use his benefits. He felt he did not deserve them as he was not injured while he was on active duty. It was common for soldiers during the 50s and 60s to not use their health benefits. Whether the process took too long, embarrassment, mental health, or just not understanding, it does not matter what age they apply for them. Only if they were honorably discharged they have them.

If your Veteran did not choose to sign up for their benefits, there is a process to get this started. You will need the Veteran's military ID number and their honorable discharge papers (**DD214 or NGB22**).

These are all things to investigate with the Veterans Office:

- Armed Forces ID card
- Discharge papers
- Date of discharge and years of duty

VA Military Attorney is available to use-

If they have not applied for or used their benefits, this can be a lengthy process, and you cannot just show up at the VA if you want to go that route. So, prepare ahead of time before they will need to use those medical benefits. A VA attorney can help you sort through what is needed to start the process and help you with any benefit suggestions, but it is unnecessary.

Were they married at the time of death?

These benefits can also cover the spouse or children of the military person. Ensure you have all spouse information, like SS#, date of birth, marriage certificate, etc. Again, you will need to provide the deceased's military branch with a death certificate and their discharge date.

There are burial benefits, and you can call your local National Cemetery regarding the process. If you are using a funeral home, they can work with the National Cemetery. They have an amazing ceremony for your loved one, and anyone can attend at no charge. If you choose not to partake, there is no obligation, and you can share what your wishes are. The spouse of the Veteran can also be buried at the same cemetery.

Veteran Home and Assisted Care-

There are times when our elders are not ready for assisted living but just need basic help at home. The VA does have programs that allow a nurse to come into the home to help with general daily grooming and tasks. They will need to apply for this, and there are qualifications that need to be met. Some of these programs have a co-pay as well, but if it's a temporary situation, they can fill that need. These programs are called VA **Home** Care and VA Home **Health** Care. The difference is that health care assistance (dispensing medications, wound care, monitoring vitals) is needed, compared to daily activities (dressing, bathing, grooming). Talking through what is needed will help assist in finding the right program.

Veteran and Survivor Benefit-

An organization called Patriot Angels was put together by Suzette Graham, former Miss Alaska. She saw the need for our wartime veterans needing assistance in their long-term care. The Veteran and/or the surviving spouse who is moving to assisted living, nursing home, or skilled care can receive a benefit from these services. Certain requirements must be met, but you can receive a $1400 minimum benefit for the Veteran's surviving spouse. If you are applying for the Veteran, the benefit amount is higher.

This is based on service and whether they served during war times. You will need your POA papers, death certificate and their actual active-duty years, marriage information, and general information like date of birth and honorable discharge papers. See the website below that can help with the requirements. Having basic information before you call will help keep the process going.

The headstone and burial are a part of their VA benefits at the National Cemetery, but you are covering how the ashes/body get there. You will also fill out the information for the headstone; they will provide you with the form ahead of time. Headstones will not be placed until you hand in the required paperwork and information, and there is a time limit to get this done.

Resources:

VA.gov Home | Veterans Affairs 12/16/2023

Patriot Angels – Leading U.S. War Heroes to a better life 12/14/2023

Assisting Families with Burial - National Cemetery Administration (va.gov) 12/14/2023

VA Survivors Pension | Veterans Affairs 2/15/2024

Charity Vehicle Donations for America's Disabled Veterans (vehiclesforveterans.org) 3/8/2024

Home Care for Veterans | A Place for Mom 3/19/2024

ORGAN DONATION

Living Organ Donor-

Anyone can become a donor, and it is completed right at the time of getting your driver's license, state ID, or renewal. My mother has never had a driver's license in all her 83 years on this earth. But we did get her a state ID, and she has that added to her identification. So that is easy and legal, but a conversation is good to have ahead of time. If the person were to die suddenly, they can prepare to use those organs with the knowledge they have. Once that is established, verify with the doctors that they have the information listed for their records. But, if the person is no longer driving and hasn't ever driven, then again, that conversation needs to be had as you cannot know their wishes, and you can't just make that decision of "yes" without any idea of what they would want to be done, this is a very personal decision, and no judgment should be made. Lastly, not all organs are viable, but it should not deter anyone from making such an unselfish gift!

Gifting your body-

To this, I also wanted to add "gifting" or "donating" your body to science. This decision needs to be made prior to death. To find an organization or university to which you would like to donate your body, a signed consent form must be completed, and a witness must be present when signing the form. Once that is established, you will arrange with them how the body will be delivered. Establishing all ahead of time ensures their wishes, you understand how the procedures work, and less confusion and wasted time. If you are an organ donor and still want to have a body gifted to science, you can still do both. The viable organs will be harvested, and they will work with the organization that you have chosen to gift the body to. The two organizations will work together to make sure the body can still be used for science. During this entire process, you will be notified; it's professional, and of course, they will keep this delicate and considerate of the sensitivity around the death. The body can still be cremated and returned to you if that is chosen to do so.

Your decision can be reversed at a later time if you choose not to go ahead.

Resources:

Organ donation after death

What's the Organ Donation Process After Death? 10 Steps | Cake Blog (joincake.com) 2/15/2023

Donation After Life | organdonor.gov 2/15/2023

Gifting your body to science

Science Care - Donate your body to science - no cost program 2/15/2023

How to Donate Your Body to Science: 11 Steps (with Pictures) (wikihow.com) 2/15/2023

DIGGING INTO CARE

Primary care-

Keeping basic contact information on their doctor, clinic, phone number, etc., can help when emergencies and prescriptions need to be taken care of and the person is not able to make those calls themselves. Adding yourself as a contact for emergencies if the medical facility needs to get a hold of the elderly is a lifesaver. My mother refers to my sisters and me a lot on her medical care, and one of us is always at an appointment with her. It is a lot of information, and she does not always understand her treatments.

Prescriptions, what pharmacy they use, and a phone number. Find out the hours, as it can be crucial when someone is in urgent need and just needs follow-up care. Some pharmacies can put you on an auto-delivery service.

What type of insurance do they have?

Asking your loved one which type of Medicare or Medicaid is important as they are different government-run insurance programs. Medicare is run by the US government. Medicaid is run by your state government and is based on your income. Some people can qualify for both!

Then, there is supplemental private insurance that works with Medicare and helps pick up costs that Medicare would not necessarily cover. The medical services that are given get billed to the supplemental insurance company, and then they work with Medicare on the balance of the amount, and they make the payment directly to the facility. So, it is important to have a copy of both cards for emergencies.

Hospitals or other medical facilities are not versed in all policies. They can vary, like staying in the network, how many days they cover, and even a private room versus shared. Have their insurance card with you on any type of visit. Sometimes, the elderly cannot admit themselves, and you will need to supply that information for them.

List of medications-

Any time after a doctor's visit is complete, have them print out a list. Then it has doses, and it's current. Do they take supplements? Add them to their medication list. Also, make sure that the meds can interact with each other. Doctors do not always have the most current information on this. Your pharmacist is a great resource—they were called a "druggist" for a reason at one time.

Talk about what they are allergic to. As we age, we develop more sensitivities to food, medications, and skin allergies. You need to know, have a list of what they are, and have them with you at appointments. Often, they cannot answer for themselves or are not even conscious. So, being prepared ahead of time can save someone's life and prevent unnecessary illnesses. Do they have hearing aids, eyeglasses, dentures, or things that the doctors and nurses need to be aware of (i.e., mom cannot hear or has dementia).

If you are the POA, bring these papers with you and have the hospital, clinic, or nursing home scan this information. I carried them with me to every type of visit I went to. Just because you gave it to the staff once does not mean they have the information, as it happens. Also, make sure you have the health care directive or living will for all types of visits. Again, different facilities and you may have to take them somewhere they have not been before. That information does not follow the patient, and they will not ask at every visit.

When being admitted to the hospital-

There are situations in which being admitted to the hospital is the best solution. Even though the doctors do not know what the diagnosis is, they may admit them as "Under Observation," and they can only stay under this admittance for so many days—the average is three. Then it is private pay! Keep checking with the doctor, as it has a financial influence. Medicare will only cover so many days; private insurance will only pick up so much of this bill. Once a diagnosis has been determined, they can change that status at any time. It is okay to ask for certain tests such as X-rays and CTC scans...it is okay to push back and ask for consults from GI and GY. Doctors are not GODS, and sometimes, it is a goose hunt trying to find the underlying cause of what is happening. All pain and physical ailments do not show themselves on the outside, and internal bleeds can be slow.... The elderly/sick person cannot push back and will just go by what is being told and agree, even though it is not what is best for them. Our elders came from a generation where doctors know everything, are authority figures, and are not to be questioned or disrespected. If it does not feel right, **ask** and **investigate**. Moving to a different hospital or health care system might seem huge, but this can all be done if you oversee that person's health care. Sometimes, you may have to pay for the transportation personally, but you may save that person's life.

Hospital Social Worker

They can assist with setting up an aftercare or home care facility, and they have lots of resources at their fingertips and at no cost to you. They are your advocates and friends. What a great resource! The social worker also knows the Medicare protocols, what is covered, and how many days they allow for aftercare, and will help with insurance questions. However, all policies are different and will only cover so many days in an aftercare facility, private room versus shared room. Once the care facility has decided you have reached your maximum exceeded days, paying out of pocket can be huge, and they charge for every service from washing clothes to having a care-person bring them back and forth to meals. Make sure you ask the social worker as many questions as possible before you leave the hospital, as they advocate for the elderly only while they are admitted there. They will help set up transportation to the care facility that is not covered by Medicare or private insurance. They have suggestions and advice as they do this daily.

"Negotiating" their care

There were times my loved ones just wanted to go home, and they were not ready, there was no one to care for them, or just too much care was needed. Dad would get angry, explosive, threatening, withdrawn, and depressed. Finding him goals to personally work towards, even if it was so outrageous and we knew he would not be able to achieve this goal, gave him something to do and look forward to. It calmed him as he knew what he was required to do. We had to bargain with him.

Have the doctor or the care team speak with them about why they cannot go home and that they are not **medically safe** to be home alone. This takes enormous pressure off you, so remember, they believe in their doctor! It is best to listen to the elderly but also not come across as shameful and treat them like they are prisoners. Talk more about their life's benefits and safety moving forward, and it may not be permanent either.

Are they a fall risk?

There is an actual name when we hang on to this couch arm, that chair back, "Furniture surfing," the elderly all know where things are in their home, so they have an unconscious routine of what to hold onto. They think they are independent, bathing, cooking, living in a clean environment, doing basic tasks. It may just be too much— driving, taking medications, it is a lot to expect others to do this for them, 24 hours a day. Falls can happen day or night, and even with a caregiver there.

Is it time to take the car keys?

Hard decision, which may not be met with agreement. Talk to the doctor privately and ask the doctor to talk with them directly. Again, they respect his professional opinion. The fact they can hurt others is not so much about them getting hurt, but others around them also. My dad drove in a 10-mile radius for many years, so he knew where everything was on a steady routine. But he was getting in all kinds of fender benders swerving, and it was difficult for him to get in and out of the car unassisted. No one wants to make these decisions as it is another sign of losing independence. But having the doctor involved and our conversations were about hurting others, he understood and gave in with no more issues.

Deciding on a nursing home, aftercare, home health care, and assisted living-

They are different and have different fees, insurance, and doctor requirements. Contact the hospital social worker to help with decisions and provide information while in the hospital. They will help set up aftercare, home care, and physical therapy, as well as help with any questions. If they have long-term care that will help them financially, let the social worker know, as that helps find a place to move them to. Skilled care is when the person cannot care for themselves at all. Their basic needs cannot be met. Assisted care can be provided by you at homecare, but while the person is still living independently. The difference is cost and coverage. Are they a renter? Do they have a clause that they can break their lease due to illness or death before the agreed-upon date?

To this, I wanted to add that when my mother decided my father just needed too much care, more than she could provide, we had to choose memory care. We could see she was burning herself out and physically exhausted. The doctors, nursing staff, and social workers can all assist in having those conversations with your loved one about not going home anymore. It is sad, hard, and disappointing, but we were worried that our mother was going to injure herself, and then what? Not everyone is upset, and since they did not make the decision, some people completely understand. We stressed safety; being "safe" was the priority. No one can argue with that!

Adult Daycare/Adult companion-

When caring for others, we must leave the house for our daily life needs and self-care. And so, there are actual places for daily "daycare" so you can do errands, make your own appointments, and just have time for yourself. They require paperwork ahead of time and the days you are looking for, and even have half days. This is an out-of-pocket expense but can be worth it, as not everyone has someone who can stay with their loved one all the time. The facilities give them meals and snacks. They provide a safe environment, with activities if they choose to participate. It is like assisted living, but you get to go home.

My aunt had hired a licensed companion to stay with her husband twice a week. They exercised and worked on memory games. It was great for her, as she could do her day without getting tired of dragging him around, and he got a different type of stimulation and challenge from another adult who had his best interest. This lasted a year and was so healthy, physically and mentally, for both. This was also an out-of-pocket expense.

Medical Alert Devices-

There are quite a few companies, and I will not go into all of them, but I will just touch on how necessary they are. Different companies do different alerts, so narrowing down your objective will help your search. We all have cell phones and cordless phones, but it is very scary when you have fallen and cannot physically reach any of those! Having this alert button around your neck means you will not be stuck without help and can communicate with someone while help is on the way. This is a paid subscription that you would set up if the person is still living independently. Many assisted living places provide medical alert devices as part of the monthly fee.

- In-home
- On the go
- Both

You can place a tracker on the cell phone and chip it in the vehicle, but if they are not driving anymore or do not have a cell phone, this will not help. But those are less expensive options and are a clever way to segue into having alerts if needed. Also, someone will have to check those devices from time to time, and that is not always dependable.

One time, falling or injuring themselves alone, and that usually makes the decision of getting this type of alert system.

Long Term Health insurance -

This is purchased from an investment firm, broker, or bank. The policy has monthly premiums that are paid and have requirements. Each policy is different, and they have been paying into this policy for years. The policy company will need to be notified when the decision has been made to move to a care facility, memory care, or assisted living facility. Long-term care will be billed first and will work with the facility and Medicare. Many recent changes have been made to these policies, and as our aging community is living longer, this type of care is extremely expensive. Please have your POA paperwork and basic info ready when you address the LTH insurance company, along with the policy contract/number.

Long-term care insurance is a policy that helps cover the costs of services not covered by regular health insurance, such as home health aide, assisted living, and nursing home care. It can help you pay for nursing home care, home health care, or assisted living if you cannot take care of yourself due to illness or disability 3. Most health and disability insurance will not cover long-term care, and those such as Medicare only cover it for a temporary period 1. Traditional long-term care policies work much like policies for auto or home insurance: you pay premiums, usually for as long as the policy is in effect, and make claims if you ever need the covered services

Bing 1/19/2024 definition

Telehealth/home care-

Once you have decided on this type of care option, your hospital social worker will set this up, prior to leaving the hospital.

They will have an individual come out within 24 hrs. and go through any electronics or medical devices and evaluate your home and how your care will work. Telehealth can assist with getting bath chairs, walkers, toilet rails, and wheelchairs. Just ask. Lift chairs are a real help when they can no longer get up on their own feet. Check with Medicare; they can assist with partial payment after a doctor signs off on this.

Sundowning-

I'm including this term because so many of our loved ones suffer from dementia in addition to other medical conditions. Their mental decline in cognitive thinking starts to become evident and can change and worsen throughout the day. Agitation, frustration, wondering are all symptoms, and even angry outbursts. My family and I found medication that helped my dad, also keeping him in a stable environment and routine, minimized those symptoms. But as our father declined, those symptoms became stronger after 4 pm. Our visits were better with him before the evening as his agitation was so high during that time we really could not have an enjoyable conversation. His memory failed, and for all of us, it was just so stressful.

This term is used in the medical field, completely describes mood, and runs parallel with the time of day. If you notice this, talk with the doctors and nurses; medications will not make it completely go away, but they will help lessen the symptoms. **Redirect** their behavior; it will help save you both when communication is at its worst. Go along with their stories, drifting. Their memories fade in and out, and correcting them just adds to the frustration and irritation.

Hospice-

Your doctor will have to put them in this "**category of health labeling**"- once it is time. Medicare steps in on paying, and if they have personal insurance. They can graduate back into normal care, too. This can switch back and forth, so do not be surprised. Your personal insurance provider will review this and keep checking in on your loved one's care with you as you are the POA, and they may even visit your loved one/ person from time to time. If a person graduates from this status, it is due to the doctor seeing improvement. I.e., weight gain, not sleeping as much, and appetite. Hospice focuses on the person and not the illness.

Having open conversations with family and friends on care, how everyone is feeling, and asking questions helps with the right decisions for your loved one and their care during this time. Texting strings are so helpful. When someone is actively dying, you cannot believe how people will change their minds and want a feeding tube, etc. Things can change because of the circumstances and go against what the individual's real wishes are.

It is okay to trade off days to visit; admit you are overwhelmed and ask for guidance.

Caring Bridge-

I come from a big family, so contacting everyone is a job. This is a great site you can set up free of charge. You can share how your loved one is doing, and they can write it or have a chosen person update it. There is no time limit on how long you can have the site or real parameters around it. It is private; you can invite those you would like to stay connected with. The greatest part of having the site is that others can respond and encourage your loved one. The only requirement is you need an email!

Personal Health Journals for Any Condition | CaringBridge 12/14/2023

WILLS/TRUSTS/HEALTH CARE DIRECTIVE

How to approach the subjects with the elder-

Suggestions while (fishing, cooking, driving) be direct, have the conversation in doses, do not interrupt, and try to let it be organic. If it is overwhelming for you, can you imagine how it is for them? Some people are not resistant; others do not want to acknowledge what is happening or simply cannot consciously relay their thoughts. However, leaving all the decisions to others gives them no control, and it is overwhelming for everyone. Be creative in how you approach these topics but do not put it off! Like any topic in life, the more you talk about it, the more comfortable you become. Even for caregivers, we do not want to think about our elders dying!

What are they:

Health Care Directive-

A living will (or instruction directive) alerts medical professionals and your family to the treatments you want to receive or refuse. In most states, this document only goes into effect if you meet specific medical criteria and are unable to make decisions. You must be 18 years of age to be a POA on a Health Care Directive. Ask your nursing home, care facility, or hospital. They usually have a form that you can fill out right there, as most of us put this off until it's completely necessary, this is only a medical POA unless it is specified for more.

Free Advance Directive Forms by State from AARP 12/11/2023

Make sure that if you have multiple people on the healthcare directive, they can make decisions independently of each other, as a decision may have to be made in an emergency situation without consulting with others. The caregivers need to have current information on you. You cannot rely on your elder to contact you when there is an emergency. Have or bring this information with you when you visit them.

Bing- 12/11/2023 definition

Do Not Resuscitate-DNR

This is a particularly important conversation and is completely voluntary. It should be talked about not only with loved ones but also with every treating doctor, and it needs to be given to the primary doctor to sign ahead of time. There are times when they are being brought into the emergency room, and a whole different doctor is attending to the elderly, and they do not know them. They do not assume their wishes. If they are unconscious, they already have protection in place for their decision. Sometimes, in emergency situations, family and friends are too emotional to make decisions, and it is less stressful to know that this is taken care of. They cannot oppose your wishes; this is a legal document. I have family that signed theirs on the way to the hospital, as it was touch and go.

DNR **means do not resuscitate.** Without a DNR, a healthcare provider will take action to revive a person who is unconscious or whose heart or breathing has stopped. A DNR means that the person does not want any life-saving measures. Resuscitation means to revive or bring back to life.

Overall, DNR orders are a complex issue that requires many ethical considerations. It is important for patients and healthcare workers to have open and honest discussions about DNR orders to ensure that everyone is on the same page and that the patient's wishes are respected.

Bing- 1/19/2024 definition

Trusts-

Trusts are created to hold and distribute assets according to the person's wishes. Having your assets in a trust means the assets can bypass probate court and are protected against money being diverted to creditors or a spouse during a divorce. Trusts offer flexibility in managing diverse types of assets and can include specific instructions for distributions, such as education expenses or homeownership.

Bing- 12/11/2023 definition

You do not have to have millions of dollars or assets to have a trust made. It is a terrific way to have everything tidy, neat, and all put together.

Make sure there is a list of beneficiaries. You can have as many as you want, with percentages listed for each one individually. Also, if you are a co-trustee, meet them! Make sure you can divide up obligations. You need to work as a team. Taking a fee vs not; and what a percentage looks like. We all have our own traits we are good at, and if one person is better at accounting and the other is a better plumber, divide and concur!

For loved ones with no children, for example, widow/widower/single, make sure it is stated what to do with the deceased body; Beneficiaries cannot make those wishes- it needs to be stated, cremation or embalmment.

(this can be added to wills trusts). Otherwise, it goes to the next of kin, and the majority decides what should be done with the body once deceased. And if it goes to the next of kin, the body is waiting for these decisions to be made, which in turn delays plans.

The attorney for the trust will establish an EIN number and give it to the trustees. Once you get this number from them, you can go ahead and set up a trust checking account to pay bills and make payments. This acts like the new estate. Taxes, bills, and deposits will all run through that new account. The other accounts are ready to close. Just make sure all payments have cleared and you have canceled any auto payments and direct deposits. When closing accounts, they will ask for death certificates and in some cases, a copy of the trust.

Wills-

Having or putting together a will is easy and can be done fast if necessary. You can obtain an estate attorney and have a will put together based on your elder's wishes. They are going to guide you through the process of taxes, covering all assets, and determining where those assets should go. They also can help with the will after the passing of a loved one, which, in turn, follows the law for your state and keeps things out of probate. I have found many sites online, for a small fee you can use, to get this done quickly and legally. Investigate which works for your loved ones, including timeline and convenience.

A will allows you to direct how your belongings—such as bank balances, property, or prized possessions—should be distributed.

Bing-12/11/2023 definition

Who is their investment broker or investment firm?

Having this information prior to their passing is important as many times, people can have a 401k they never cashed out or rolled over. They can have accounts at more than one financial facility, so reaching out to these various places will be a lot easier with the contact information. They do not have to share balances or personal information; just getting the information about where the accounts are will help if you need to get to funds quickly. You may have to use those funds to pay bills, and you will need to give them the POA paperwork if the elderly have not. Just like they will need a copy of the trust or will. They can guide you through the process. The financial advisor is not an accountant, so it is an initiative-taking idea to get the accountants' information they have used or use your own accountant.

There can be tax consequences, so having the advisor and accountant involved together is helpful when dissolving funds. Even after you die, you still pay taxes!

Retirement accounts-

The beneficiaries will have an account set up with their own social security number after the person passes, or if there are multiple beneficiaries, they will set up a "beneficiary" account and disperse funds through that account. Each beneficiary must provide a social security number, date of birth, and basic contact information.

You can choose to keep the deceased funds and have those funds, or your percentage transferred "in kind" to where you have your assets held, or cash out the assets and receive full payment. This is all based on tax brackets and your state taxes. Some accounts will be easy to close because of the federal requirements—it can vary from state to state, and our tax laws change constantly. You will also have to decide if you want the estate to pay the taxes or if you want the individual beneficiary to cover their portion after the deceased person dies. Talking with an accountant can help guide you in what is best for you.

Life insurance-

I have added this at the end of this chapter, as this is not paid out until after the passing, but it is crucial to know, as policies vary- and they can be set up through a bank, credit union, or employer, not just an insurance company. The insured has been paying a monthly payment, so watch that on their banking statements. You will need to have beneficiary information and the death certificate. If no beneficiary is listed or alive, then it goes to a contingent beneficiary; if there is not one or they are not living anymore, then it can go to probate, and the courts decide.

Again, it is crucial to make sure these policies are up to date. Often, when the insured signed up years ago, they never looked at it again. Money from a life insurance policy is as good as cash for inheritance because it also is not taxable by the IRS. But again, state tax laws can change and vary from year to year.

Cremation Policy-

This policy can be purchased through a funeral home and is considered an asset. The policy is wonderful to have, as their funeral expenses are paid upfront and do not come out of the estate balance. The elderly can plan their funeral and direct how the money should be spent. They can direct on how much for flowers, programs, all the details they would like. If you do not spend the full purchase amount for the policy, you will get the difference back.

The funeral home will keep the policy on record and give the policy owner a copy for future reference. If your loved one is on county assistance, this policy is considered an asset, and some states have a maximum on their total worth. It is a one-time payment, and everything is done! You can choose to use a different funeral home, then where they bought the policy, you will work with them on making that change.

Taxes

This is important as we all have to pay our taxes and no matter what age, doing someone else's is challenging! In the files you set up, I suggest having a separate file for the different receipts, statements, and notes that come over the year and need to be dealt with when filing. Guess what? This makes having them in one spot easy, and now we are not hunting for them! As we age, what qualifies and gets taxed has different laws and requirements. It is difficult to know what will pertain to their filing, as these vary per state, and the government is always changing what a deduction is and what is not.

If they rent, they can file for a "renters rebate." Do they need to take mandatory IRA distributions? Is their social security taxed? Do they have other sources of income? Mortgage interest? Do they make charitable contributions? A lot of this will mirror your own taxes, but you still need to have the exact information. We chose to use my aunt's accountant, and I had been in touch with him throughout the year as we were handling her estate. He was aware of the distributions being made to the beneficiaries and what her trust may have to pay out.

Currently, there are tax deductions on some assisted living care expenses if they are in a qualified facility. You need to have these statements showing what is paid out. An assisted living care facility gives you those itemized statements, so keep those monthly statements.

Some examples of what they could deduct are:

- Medication Management
- Bathing
- Medical equipment

*I want to note that the payment for their actual "living" at the assisted living or memory care facility is **not** tax-deductible, but it is the add-ons of additional care that can be tax deductible.

Resources:

Is Assisted Living Tax Deductible? | A Place for Mom 3/11/2024

Tax Deductions for Assisted Living Costs (elderlawanswers.com) 3/11/2024

Medical, Nursing Home, Special Care Expenses | Internal Revenue Service (irs.gov) 3/11/2024

HARD MEDICAL DECISIONS

Deciding on no more medical care-

It is okay to decide; no more dental appointments, surgeries, or even medications. Sometimes, our loved one tells us without saying words. **Quality of life over quantity.** Sometimes we come to a place of being tired, resistant, frustrated with treatments, poking, prodding, and just feeling weak. Having a DNR in place helps when it is escalated to an emergency, but this decision is quite different. It is personal!

If all medical treatment has been exhausted, your next step is palliative care or hospice. This can be at a hospice facility, at home, or at the nursing home where they are currently staying. You decide either with that person, loved ones, the doctor, and/or the social worker. The social worker will help you plan if you choose to die at home—meaning, having oxygen sent to your home, nurse visits, how to administer pain meds, hospital bed, and they will arrange to come pick everything up once it is no longer needed. If you choose a hospice facility, they will arrange to have them placed comfortably. Hospice will then take over all of the care and work with you and the person who is dying on how that will look. You can bring pictures, play music, bring their favorite things—it is about comfort. Many hospice facilities have isolated areas where you can stay the night and dining rooms that provide meals for loved ones. They cater to all of you - it is really a peaceful and caring environment. They offer comfort, peace, and support for others while administering care to their loved ones. Hospice is about treating the person and not the illness. True earth angels!

What these terms are-

Palliative Care-

Palliative care is an interdisciplinary medical caregiving approach aimed at optimizing the quality of life and mitigating suffering among people with serious, complex, and often terminal illnesses.

Microsoft Bing-12/11/2023

Hospice-

Hospice care is a type of health care that focuses on the palliation of a terminally ill patient's pain and symptoms and attending to their emotional and spiritual needs at the end of life. This type of care can go on for days, weeks, and even a year. My father graduated out of hospice as he was improving at times.

Microsoft Bing-12/11/2023

Death Doula-

A trained professional who provides emotional, physical, and educational support for someone nearing death. They can be considered a mentor for the last chapter of life and are typically brought in by the dying individual's family 3. The services offered by an end-of-life doula could include a mix of the following:

- Providing the opportunity to talk openly and honestly about the dying process.

- Alleviating the anxiety, guilt, and shame often associated with death.
- Helping to create a peaceful and comfortable environment for the dying person.
- Providing support to the dying person's family and friends.
- Assisting with practical tasks such as funeral planning and paperwork.

Death doulas work together with palliative care and hospice teams, and this is exactly what you can expect when hiring an end-of-life doula. The role of a death doula is to help facilitate what the person and their family need, using spiritual and homeopathic practices.

What fits your needs and comfort? There are times when you have weeks to decide on care and other times when decisions must be made quickly. So, talking about a plan ahead of time sure makes the grieving process a little lighter. As far as hospice, this type of care can go on for days, weeks, and up to a year. A friends father graduated in and out of hospice, a few different times as he was improving.

Microsoft Bing- 12/11/2023

ACTIVELY DYING

When it is decided that no more treatments can be done, the disease has progressed too far, or just signs of the body shutting down, this is a whole new stage you are entering. The elderly have been processing what is next, and your thoughts are completely different than theirs. The 'living' concentrates on living without them and the hole that is left. The dying concentrate on the present; it is their time, sometimes fear. This can be difficult to witness, but our feelings need to be set aside, as they are dying, and they have given this much thought.

The body starts to shut down, and we basically stop eating, taking water, and can hallucinate. And this can be hard to observe, as we want them to have nourishment, but the body knows. Asking, prodding, and making them feel guilty for not taking one more bite is just causing stress for both of you. Let us just let them have what **they** want.

Their body can also start to change color, pale greyish. It is part of the process. They can become unresponsive. But that does not mean they cannot hear you or feel your touch. My father was not talking anymore, but he sure reacted when we touched his feet! They can have a raspy sound or gurgle to their breathing (death rattle). Some may opt to provide oxygen, but we chose no more as he hated all the medical devices he was hooked up to. We wanted him to be comfortable and loved and know he was safe and not alone.

While all of this is happening, you will have nurses and a doctor checking vitals and giving morphine. Morphine can help with the struggles of breathing, at a small dose, and even with any pain and anxiety. I watched my aunt struggle to breath, and she felt like she couldn't get a deep breath. Morphine took that anxiety away, calmed her, and she was more settled. It is difficult to watch someone struggle, and certainly at this time when there is no more fighting. There should be no discomfort, so why not help them through this process and be comfortable.

During this period, we called loved ones who could not be there to say goodbye. We actually held the phone up to my dad's ear. It was so healing and beautiful, and it was a gift to know you are loved. Hold their hand, touch them, talk to them, take pictures. You can play their favorite music and watch their favorite show or sports. There does not have to be a somber, sad, quite way to be with someone when they pass. My close friend made her mother her favorite food, and everyone who came to say goodbye got to delight in a meal, some stories, and the real beauty of witnessing a loving moment. We want to be careful not to pass on our fears. Our fears of the unknown or project our beliefs. It is about that person and their feelings and thoughts.

In my research, I read an interview with a hospice nurse who said that she would frequently get asked, "I don't know what to say." "I don't know if they can hear me," her advice is quite simple, she said, "say the following":

- I am here for you
- I love you
- I will be okay
- Thank you

The rest will come on its own. You may have a few minutes, hours, or no time, but those four phrases cover plenty!

Right after they pass, the funeral home of your choosing will need to be called. Then, the funeral home picks up the body. You can wait and be present there. They will help with your wishes and give you a timeline of the days ahead. You can visit them before they get cremated; just contact the funeral home. Lastly, friends and relatives have asked for a thumb print for future use. They have taken this thumbprint and had a pedant made, tattoo, or just for their personal keepsake. It may sound morbid, but you may be relieved to have it after the sadness wears off.

The funeral home will prepare and order the death certificates - (5 originals are plenty). There is a fee for these, which varies per state. Not all businesses want to have the originals or a copy anymore. We are in a digital area, so they scan a copy and give it back- just like trusts and wills, the funeral home will want a copy—have digital copies scanned for yourself and given to other trustees or beneficiaries. Still, a few paper copies are very necessary. If the deceased has a cremation policy with the same funeral home, then the policy starts to kick in, and they will have all that information already set up and start putting those funds towards their fees.

-Giving ourselves and sharing experiences instead of "things" is the best way to live out what time you have with your loved one.

PLANNING AFTER THE PASSING

This is a very emotional time, as you have been involved in care physically with this person, and now they are gone. The time and space going forward is about "dismantling" their life now. The Power of Attorney ends the day the person passes, and beneficiary and any legal designation takes over, like a Transfer on Death or TOD. If there is a Trust or Will that comes into effect and replaces the POA. The most current paperwork is what is legal, so if amendments were made, you should go by the most current date.

By now, you have knowledge of bank accounts, cash, and other assets, and having a meeting with the beneficiary/s is a wonderful way to start so everyone is on the same page and understands what you may need from them, and of course, hopefully getting emotional and physical support for what is ahead.

Caution: Medicare and Social Security will not call you—ever. So, make sure these are some of your first calls to discontinue.

Funeral homes-

Once you have decided to use a funeral home, they have funeral planners (just like a wedding planner). Use them to help facilitate and set appointments and get things together with your church or facility. They will collaborate with you on your needs and expenses, and some will charge a fee. You can order flowers through them; they will ensure they are delivered and placed if other people have bought plants and flowers. They will bring the ashes/body for you to where the afterlife event is taking place, from the funeral home. They can help with music, live streaming, and rituals of the church they are versed in. They will take care of the programs, with your direction of who and what you want. Some churches can serve food afterward, such as a luncheon. There are separate fees for a pastor from the church.

You can also just get the ashes and decide what you want at another time. Some churches do not perform a celebration of life. You also need to be a member of some churches to have a funeral. Contact the church director. You can have your plans made ahead of time with the elder—songs, readings, who is participating in the funeral. These are all amazing conversations you can have, and really a time to share and learn about who they are, their accomplishments, wants, needs, and likes. You do not have to make these decisions right away.

Flying with ashes-

Three things are required when flying with the cremated remains on a domestic flight.

- Cremated remains must be carried on board and cannot be checked.
- Cremated remains must be in a container that can be x-rayed.
- Lastly, the Certificate of Cremation (official document produced by the crematory) must accompany cremated

remains. , your Pastor/Priest/Minister can also sign papers for the release of ashes.

Microsoft Bing-12/11/2023 definition TSA regulations site

Cremated Remains | Transportation Security Administration (tsa.gov)

Alternative Cremation-

We are all on a different journey, and a traditional funeral or cemetery plot might not be where you want to have a final resting place. We are in a world of many choices and beliefs. You can choose to have your ashes in a biodegradable urn planted with a tree. You can even make crystals with the ashes, called a "spirit piece." They can work with the funeral home, and you send the kit to them. That piece or urn can be used for a celebration of life. Amazon and Etsy have many options for urns. This is such a personal time, so do not let your decisions be based on what has been done before!

PREPARING YOUR FILE SYSTEM

Where to start after your loved one has passed and you are ready to take over!

Whether on paper or electronically, you must have copies and originals of legal papers, bills, death certificates, and assets. Where is their wallet, social security card, and driver's license? See, this is basic but particularly valuable information, etc. Having a system surely helps. Set yourself up so you know where this basic information is. You will be asked the date of birth and the date of passing every time! You will say these numbers and dates like a robot. But until then, you need to have this information readily available. You will use a lot of the same information, like address, social security number, date of birth, etc. However, that works for you, a spreadsheet, notebook, files. I had written all of this basic information in front of a folder, so I was prepared.

- Personal (Credit Cards, Insurance, Banking)

- Legal (Wills, Beneficiary, Trust)
- Medical (Dr, Clinics, Care facilities)
- Taxes

You will need to cancel subscriptions, insurance policies, and household utilities. Going through their banking statements will help a lot, as you will get an idea of what gets paid monthly. Keep a record of when you called to cancel and to whom you spoke. Many times, you will get reimbursement for the unused days. Sometimes, we must keep the heat on until the house is sold, but there is a lot of money to be saved by cutting the cable and newspaper right away.

If they have a Trust or Will, set up two regulated "worksheets," Excel will be your friend. This will be sent to all beneficiaries every time funds are disbursed. One spreadsheet shows assets the day the person passes. (Car, home, boat, accounts) etc. The other worksheet will show what is coming in and out of their accounts after they pass, as well as their balances.

Please see my examples at the end of this chapter.

When there is a trust, the attorneys can assist with the legal side of an estate. They may charge a 1% fee for the total assets when the person passes. They will set up the EIN number on the trust, and you will need this number when selling real estate, opening a trust bank account, and selling investments. This ensures the taxes are not completed under the deceased's social security number. You can also negotiate the amount of work and who will do what with the attorney's office.

At any time, a beneficiary can ask for information/accounting on what is being spent and done with assets. So, you must keep accurate records of this information. Keeping totals of what comes in and what goes out, dates, who to and for what...fixing the sink, doctors bill, light bill, deposits, selling personal assets (furniture, HH, etc.) all those assets/money runs through the trust account you just opened. This will be added to your trust worksheet. You will have to keep monthly statements, receipts, and deposits. You will also need to keep this information for taxes. Not everything is taxed, but you will have to have the taxes done for the final year they were alive and while there are still assets that belong to the trust.

The trustee can decide on a fee to charge the trust as a trustee. It can vary; what is your time worth? Driving, appointments, gas, calls, mail, copies, this comes from the real estate balance, but you are managing all of it. The average person charges $70.00 to $80.00 an hour. The attorney represents "The Trust." You are the keeper of the trust executor/trustee...when signing anything pertaining to the trust, bills, mortgage, checks, or legal papers, you will sign YOUR name and put TTE afterward. Remember to use the EIN number from the trust when filling out real estate forms or any tax forms. Any income that generates 1099 will be reported to the IRS. It gets to be confusing because that person is no longer here, but the "Trust" is responsible for the taxes.

ASSET BALANCES DAY OF THE DEATH

Name	Type	Valuation Date	Account Number	Value*
Bank	Checking Account			
Bank	Savings Account			
Investment	IRA Account			
Investment	Personal Investment (CD, Annuity)			
	Camper/Trailer			
	Vehicle			
	Personal Property (Jewelry, Household, Guns)			
Trust Bank (new acct)	TRUST Checking Account: = Trustees			
			TOTAL DOD Value of Estate:	

		Deceased Checking Account				
Date	Deposits	Description	Withdrawals	Chk#		Balance*
		Beginning Balance				
		Ending Balance				
			Balance			

		Deceased Savings Account				
Date	Deposits	Description	Withdrawals	Chk#		Balance*
		Beginning Balance				
		Ending Balance				
			Balance			

		Deceased IRA Account				
Date	Deposits	Description	Withdrawals	Chk#		Balance*
		Beginning Value				
		Ending Value				
			Balance			

		Deceased Investment Account				
Date	Deposits	Description	Withdrawals	Chk#		Balance*
		Beginning Value				
		Ending Value				
			Balance			

*Once you set up the new account with the EIN number, you can just copy and paste your DOD accounting spread sheet for the on-going period of tracking of expenses and assets. Prepare for a good year, with closing accts, setting up accts, selling property, taxes, etc.

PLEASE NOTE: These are just sample documents, which contain summarized information and is not intended to include comprehensive details regarding day-to-day market performance, minimal expenses, and other minor transactions. Pursuant to A.R.S. 14-11005, any objections regarding your accounting or action associated with they must be presented within one (1) year.

You are responsible for reporting your distributive share of the post-death taxable income, deductions, credits, etc., of the estate assets on your individual tax returns for any year in which a distribution is received. If you have questions about how distributions from the Trust will impact on your individual tax liability, please consult your tax professional.

ASSETS

When it is time to sell their home, vehicle, and belongings.

The nagging voice says it is time to sell and find a realtor. You will need one who is patient, direct, and driven. Realtors have many contacts—electricians, plumbers, and contractors. Sometimes, having 5k of work done to the home will profit the estate a lot, so have them help and hire whomever to get this done. We sold my aunt's property and then sold some of her household items to the buyers in a separate transaction. They wrote me a check after our closing, and it worked—smoothly! As there were fewer items for which we had to find a new home. A good realtor can help facilitate this type of transaction and will do so with no fee. It is a big undertaking as older pieces of property can have a lot of deferred maintenance, and you may just need to sell the home or property as is. Your agent has contacts to use and remember he/she wants to get the best price, so work together.

You will have to fill out the disclosures on the property, so keep the mortgage, property tax information, and any household paperwork available. Please ask your realtor questions; they are professionals, licensed, and educated on what is happening with the market. Waiting a few months can be painful financially at that time, but it can change when it is the right market to sell after the holidays or springtime. If your loved one is unable to help with selling, remember it is still their home, and communicating with them about the details will help them feel less anxious about such a huge loss of their livelihood. Not only is it hard to move into a care facility with strangers, but they also have to say goodbye to their home, with all its security and comfort! For the homes I sold, we cleaned out all the clutter, removed personal photos, and ensured there was curb appeal. It is work, but overall, it paid off with three offers in one day. We then could focus on the rest of the items in the home and close that chapter.

Let's add, do they have a mortgage? This is a suitable time to call the mortgage company and ask for a "forbearance" so you can save what they have in checking and savings and not make the mortgage payment anymore. The person has passed, and the home will be up for sale. You have now given yourself and the estate at least 90 days to get the home on the market and sell and use the mortgage payment amount for other bills or necessary updates to the home.

If they have a reverse mortgage, you will need to notify the mortgage or bank of what is happening. The reverse mortgage may have paid them in a lump sum, or they receive payments. When the home is sold, that will be paid back. The title company will help explore this information before it is sold.

The stuff!

Using the home or property as a command center keeps things centrally located and has everyone come together to make decisions. Deciding on someone's belongings is massive! I have found giving myself breaks or time limits while sorting and packing up someone else's belongings was easier. Bad decisions can be made when we are tired, burnt out, and well, just sad. You are grieving for a person who is no longer living there, and it is time-consuming—mentally and physically. And well, it HAS TO BE DONE. There are companies you can hire and who will pack up a household and pay you for what they think it is worth. There are estate companies, and while they do the work, you get a percentage of what is sold. We had an auction for my parents. The auction company took everything off the property and combined the sale with other estates. At the end of the auction, they took a percentage, cut me a check, and everything was gone; talk about not thinking! All the work was done in a day, and there was no heavy lifting. There are choices, and it depends on how much you think your time is worth.

The personal side of going through your loved one's belongings is very private and almost feels intrusive at times. But it is needed. I found it cathartic and explained more about who that person was at a deeper level. Set a goal, "Today I am cleaning out this room," or "this desk." Sometimes, cleaning out a certain cabinet is too emotionally painful, so asking someone else to do it is so healthy!

Give yourself some grace. You are unraveling someone else's life. There were times I had some big laughs to myself, opening another cabinet full of Christmas items. Ask for help! Not only friends and family but churches, shelters, and childcare facilities need household items for their clients and will come to pick up clean and useful items. Social media has several sites where you can list items. It is a fantastic way to move things along without having to run around and keep quality items out of our landfills.

Digital Platforms (legacy)

This is a digital world; yes, even our elderly use social media, and so many of us have more than one account. What do we do with these platforms? Should we carry on, delete, and freeze the accounts and run? This is a strange conversation, but it is necessary, as this is how we communicate with so many of our loved ones.

I have so many pictures, videos, and contacts set up on mine; it is a mini legacy and a holding place of my life. There is marriage, kids, grandchildren, hardship, and my pets! Think about this ahead of time; talk about what should be done with email and phone numbers. I have received emails back stating: "This email is no longer in use," and a forwarding email was given. I have seen an announcement on Facebook pages to say goodbye as the person has passed and will no longer have an active page. In the big picture, this may seem like no big deal, but eventually, it will be, as it can be just too painful to manage people emailing and messaging about what happened or asking about the person.

Either way, discuss this when you can; it will set you up later, so you will not have to think about how to respond to questions.

PROCESSING, GRIEVING, AND THE FUTURE

When we are caregiving, we spend time, mentally and physically **"doing"** for that person. We are all about therapies, medication, doctors, insurance, and then it is— silence! Life takes a different shift after they pass. It is less thinking, doing, and managing someone's life, and then it goes to solitude. The time we used to spend in our minds figuring out their day-to-day, now that time is available for other things, it is an adjustment. During our caregiving time, we do not think about ourselves, but just in a way that I will do this when I have time. When will I get to that? It is time. It is doing mundane things. It is resting our body and mind and just breathing in real-time. I call it **"just being!"** It is okay to feel lonely, resentful, confused, and relieved! We just need to feel it, breathe, and learn to value what we were a part of.

I think about all the loved ones I have had in my life which have passed. Not every day, but when I see a bird, smell the rain, when the 4th of July comes, I can get sad, I can laugh, and I certainly get melancholy for them. But I do know that I am so blessed to have been allowed to share time with them, to be taught by them, to laugh and even cry with them. I know I am a better person because of my experiences with them, and I was able to learn love, compassion, and friendship. And all of our years on earth, **"living,"** isn't that a huge gift? Isn't that what it is to be a great human? Thank you to everyone that I have lost. I wish you could see me today; I know each of you is writing with me as I work on this guide. Please feel your grief in your own way, and really be patient!

Learning what a new normal will look like will take time, tears, frustration, and hair-pulling! Working through feelings, or not, and putting them aside so you can get through dinner is typical, but we need to move, no matter how big the step is. There are still tasks that need to be handled, people to meet with, and work to go back to.

This is all happening while you just lost a significant person in your life. It's okay! There were times I wanted to yell in the grocery store aisle, "Hey, everyone, my best friend just died today!" But we should not do that, at least not in the store. Allowing yourself to find **"you"** again is what your loved one wants you to do. To live and love your life. Make plans, do things, enjoy your life, and **"not live your life like a run-on sentence."** Get a haircut, learn a new skill, go hiking, travel to a new place, and share with your loved one you are okay and resilient.

This is hard to share, as there are times I still cry, but I hold onto them dearly, and I have no problem talking to them aloud and saying, I love you, you are missed!

SUGGESTIONS

Who wants to hear these tidbits? Like, I know enough...but these are just little snippets!

YOUR Loved One-

Hmmm, try not to shame your loved one. We get frustrated and tired, but how we "say it" comes through more than what we "are saying." Encouragement is key to recovery and everyday living. Give them accolades even if they have only eaten once that day!

Let them answer the questions; when asked by PT, DR, and nurses—we want to answer for them, but it is a fantastic way to check their comprehension. You do not have to answer them because they look at you; give it a minute; I am thinking and searching for the right words.

Engage and give goodwill to the nurses and people who care for our loved ones. Be interested in them. They are vigilantly helping your loved one and developing a trusting relationship with them. You are not with them all the time, and the caregiver/nurses appreciate your interest in them. It is an emotional, demanding job.

*****

Once it is time to move to a facility, ask if they will waive signing fees or part of the month's rent if you are moving in with 10 days left of the month. You would be surprised how accommodating they can be.

What is the ratio of patients to nurses? Can they dispense medications? How many times do they interact or check on your loved one?

Ask yourself, would I live here? Is it clean, friendly, and safe? Is there enough to do? Are residents involved?

Can they keep a vehicle? Do they have garage stalls or their own storage lockers?

Put their names on everything! Permanent marker on the label, as things get lost easily! We found the inside sleeve works also.

Personal belongings-

Take notice of expensive items, money, jewelry, and electronics that should not be left in the care of a sick/dying loved one. Sometimes, these things can go missing, and you will not get them back.

Downsizing-

Maybe they are not ready to leave their home, but you can give them tasks to help with all of the items. They can donate, throw, or keep. No one needs 15 coffee cups anymore or 10 tape measures. Getting them actively involved in a cupboard or desk can help with your own peace of mind. And reasoning with them that this is a lot to just leave for someone else.

*****

Help them with simple tasks, like opening boxes and carts to carry items and help with deliveries. Those simple tasks can help them when living alone. Often, they see you helping with so many chores and will not ask for help with the simplest tasks.

Bring them things to do, crossword puzzles, books, coloring books, mind activities, cards, and photo albums. Sometimes, they cannot read anymore, but downloading audiobooks or podcasts can bring so much joy! Having an active mind and using your brain keeps us healthier and active.

Be creative in helping your loved one live with their illness or aging. Red is the last color a dementia patient can recognize, so using that color to flag where the bathroom is very effective. Sticky notes on cupboards, days of the week posted in large letters, and number prescriptions on the caps so they know what order to take meds. Working with what they can understand is half the battle.

Cellphones/laptops/chargers/reading glasses/hearing aid chargers are needed when they stay somewhere and do not forget them when they leave!

Facetime! Just another way to be with them when you cannot be physically there. Aides can help if they are not certain how to set that up on the phone. Zoom calls are another wonderful way to get others together. They are free, up to a certain time limit, and people can dial in from anywhere.

Ask about bringing treats or their favorite goodies such as soda, things that have the comforts of home, a favorite blanket, and pictures. Can you bring your dog to visit? Most places have no problem with these visits. This is a huge alert, *but nuts can be very harmful if your loved one has issues with swallowing, which can lead to aspiration pneumonia. Those types of choices can be harmful.

Day trips-

Many care facilities have requirements when taking them away for a day or two. They do not provide transportation but need your plan. They need to provide medications, cancel physical therapy, and make changes to their daily schedule. The care facility is not responsible for the person once they have left their residence and are in your care.

*****

Certainly, contact your church- Minister/Pastor for visits. Some have days they will give communion and will help guide them in their time of need. They will come to the care facilities and even anoint the sick or administer last rites for the dying.

Volunteers-

Many facilities have volunteers once they are in hospice. They come to read to them, play cards, and just interact with them. My dad had visits by a wonderful woman, and she would read him the sports page and go over our local team sports news. He was not reading anymore, but someone came in and gave him an hour once a week. You cannot always be there, but it's okay!

Many hospice facilities will give grievance counseling to you and the family once the person has passed for up to a year at no charge. Use this service. Being a caregiver can bring all kinds of new life adjustments once they are gone. Grieving can sneak up on you at any time.

*****

What me!

Have your own snacks and beverages for yourself. Cafeterias close, and stores are not open at late hours. Keep a sweater on hand. You may catch yourself visiting at odd times and need to take care of your own needs.

Take care of yourself during and after. It is okay to set boundaries around your time...it can be depressing, scary, and frustrating, but it also can be a cherished time with that person and a chance to heal some old wounds.

Lastly, there were some long hours at the hospital waiting on tests from doctors and just staying with my loved one. I found walking the hospital or the grounds cleared my head and gave me a different perspective at times. There are some beautiful gift shops, and I have made some fun purchases!

I found doing the easiest stuff first or the basic daily chores helped put one foot in front of the other!

FULL CIRCLE

This is a lot of information, many shared experiences, references, and some hard memories I have put together for you. I just wanted people to know that death is another extension of life. You love and respect this person who has passed, but you will find you will know them more intimately, including secrets. You are really putting someone to bed forever! I found old pictures that my friend had said she had gotten rid of; I feel it was just too painful for her to see them again, and she had said goodbye to those times or that life that was long ago.

When we are caregiving for a loved one, we are in the thick of it—their life, their needs, their wishes, and it's hard not to feel resentful because we haven't done our own personal discovery because there is always time, it's depressing, and it's not going to happen for a long time. But it does; like the saying, taxes, and death are a for sure thing! So, in that process, chipping away at it to make it easier for others and us makes all those feelings a reality and somewhat managed. We all have some control over what we leave behind.

Do not live your life in panic, **"Is this the big one?" "I can't eat that, or I'll have a stroke!"** We do not have to live in this kind of paranoia, which is not living. But being honest and forthright about how you are cared for sure helps in situations as they arise. There is a lot of information on the web, organizations, and professionals you can get help from, but if you have a starting point, a place that moves you from hiding about dying to bringing out conversations with others, doesn't that make those voices, slow done, and not so loud?

We can all do the hard stuff. You are going to cry, there might be fights, and doors may get slammed. I went through a lot of that with other family members and with the dying person. My aunt would have me repeat back to her the notes that I was taking down. I was seriously frustrated, but I did it and got through those feelings. I laugh at it now! My dad did not want his ashes placed at the family lake- as he put it, he did not want to "dirty the water." But we had subtle conversations, and I am sure he did not even realize that these little nuggets were gold!

There are a lot of guides on birth, living, and relationships, and they give us a path, a push; this is the same; it is just about a hard subject for everyone that is involved! I do know that not everyone is afraid or in denial; a great friend of mine has picked out her music and readings. Her faith leads her to make decisions while she lives her best life!

Lastly, my experiences are my education. I do not have a degree, I do not have a legal background, or a medical license, I have just been through plenty of complex situations with loved ones. I had family and friends pass, and I was there to witness their journey. And each time it stayed with me- it called me. So, I had to get this out of my mind and out to the universe.

And by the way, it's -10 out, and it was a beautiful sunny day!

MY RESOURCES

My resources have been personally helping several family and friends go through this challenging stage of life. I also worked in banking, investments, and HR for 30 years. Searching the web, listening to podcasts, and reading blogs have helped broaden my knowledge. Talk to your own banker, accountant, and other professionals for advice, and most of them you already know can help with your situation.

Elder Attorney

They will give a free consultation and help start with a plan of action. I suggest using one, as they can work with the county if the loved one needs financial assistance. A lot of paperwork is needed, and when working with the county, the elder attorney will make sure the paperwork is complete and accurate. They will work with the county social workers to ensure they are actively working on the case and staying up to date on any changes.

The financial state of the loved one is the significant reason you will need county help if you decide on an aftercare facility or long-term care. The elder attorney can also set up a Trust, Will, and POA. They are not required, but they sure speed things up!

Elder Attorneys & Lawyers Near You 2/15/2023

Care Giving

Finding a paid care giver if they are able to live at home.

Care.com 12/11/2023

Providing Care and Comfort at the End of Life | National Institute on Aging (nih.gov) 3/8/2024

AARP

Looking for advice, discounts, and even jobs & education? AARP has all kinds of articles and videos on everything you need to know about aging! I used to make fun of getting their letters in the mail, but now I am impressed with the information they put out.

AARP® Official Site - Join & Explore the Benefits 12/11/2023

Selling property

My husband is a licensed contractor and realtor. Not only was he the trustee of his own mother's trust, but he has also helped many clients rehab their homes and then sell their loved ones' homes for the best price. Sometimes, that is their only asset, and every penny counts when you go into a nursing home or assisted living.

Home-Selling Checklist: 12 Things To Do Before Selling Your House (realtor.com) 2/15/2024

Care Providers:

Qualified Facilities for services, nursing homes, assisted living facilities, hospice. There are over 15,000 certified nursing homes throughout the country.

Medicare.gov- lots of information throughout their pages

Compare Care Near You | Medicare 12/15/2023

What Are Palliative Care and Hospice Care? | National Institute on Aging (nih.gov) 3/8/2024

Hospice Foundation Of America - Signs of Approaching Death- 3/8/2024

What Are Death Doulas? (webmd.com) 3/8/2024

A Place for Mom

This company helps you find a care facility at no charge. They work with your criteria. I personally used this company, and it is impressive!

touring-checklists.pdf (aplaceformom.com) 3/8/2024

APFM Newsletter Short Lead Form (aplaceformom.com) 12/15/2023

CaringBridge

A great and easy site- I cannot emphasize enough; use it!

Personal Health Journals for Any Condition | CaringBridge 12/15/2023

Social Security office-

Benefits, survivor benefits, Medicare information.

The United States Social Security Administration | SSA 1/1/2024

General Guidance-

Six questions to ask that will make caring for older relatives much easier (msn.com) 3/8/2024

Retirees' Anti-Bucket List: 10 Experiences You Don't Want (msn.com) 3/8/2024

Actively Dying Articles-

End-Of-Life Workers Are Sharing The Major Things We Get Wrong About Death (msn.com) 2/20/2024

Home Five Wishes

Go Wish – Coda Alliance

Dementia Society of America | Information Support Research 3/8/2024

The End

Made in the USA
Monee, IL
18 January 2025

10211989R00069